Come live with me

LOIS
WYSE

American Greetings Corporation
Cleveland, Ohio 44144

Published by American Greetings, American Road, Cleveland, Ohio 4414
First printing, June, 1971. Copyright, 1971, by Lois Wyse.
Library of Congress Catalogue Card Number: 78-157556
Printed in the United States of America
An American Greetings Book

for you

Cross Currents

Do not skip stones
On the river of my love.
Cross currents
Are at work.

Don't Turn Back

Friendship can turn to love,
But how sad the love
That turns to
Friendship.

Self-confidence

I know today
Is what I make it.
So why do I check my horoscope?

Come Live with Me

The only problem
In living with someone
Is that you assume
You know that person totally.

"In" Love

To be in fashion
Is to be in love
With one's own time.

Hello, Wizard

Whatever became
Of the yellow brick road?

What is Immoral Now?

I define immorality as
Injustice,
Corruption,
And unreasonable demands
On the soul of a man
In the name of love.

I Grant You Three Wishes

If everything you wish
Has come to pass,
You did not wish for very much.

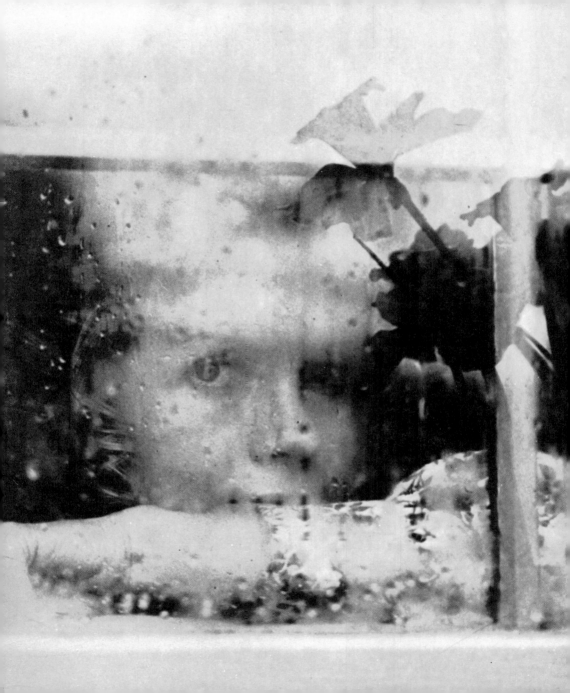

The Falseness of Truths

The truest truths
Are fantasies.

In Harmony

I believe in peace.
But I know there can be
No peace in the world
Until one man and one woman
Can live together
In harmony.

X Rating

Movies are dirtier than ever,
But still they are not
As sordid as life.

For Once

We came very close
To love
And so I guess I'm grateful
That even though I didn't catch
The brass ring
I came very close.

For once.

A special dedication . . . To Rob, who helped

The Author

Lois Wyse is the author of best-selling books of
love poetry, including "Love Poems For The Very Married",
"Are You Sure You Love Me?", and "I Love You Better Now",
as well as the popular non-fiction book, "Mrs. Success".
Her articles and poems appear regularly in numerous
magazines in the United States and abroad.

Lois Wyse, her husband Marc, and their two children,
Katherine and Robert, live in Shaker Heights, Ohio.